Punctuation
A guide for editors and proofreaders

Gerard M-F Hill

First published in the UK in 2021 by
Chartered Institute of Editing and Proofreading
Apsley House
176 Upper Richmond Road
London
SW15 2SH

ciep.uk

Copyright © 2021 Chartered Institute of Editing and Proofreading

ISBN 978 1 915141 02 6 (print)
ISBN 978 1 915141 03 3 (PDF ebook)

All rights reserved. No part of this publication may be reproduced or used in any manner without written permission from the publisher, except for quoting brief passages in a review.

The moral rights of the author have been asserted.

The information in this work is accurate and current at the time of publication to the best of the author's and publisher's knowledge, but it has been written as a short summary or introduction only. Readers are advised to take further steps to ensure the correctness, sufficiency or completeness of this information for their own purposes.

Developmental editing, copyediting and proofreading by CIEP members
Cathy Tingle, Margaret Hunter, Jacqueline Harvey, Bev Sykes

Typeset in-house
Original design and punctuation graphics by Ave Design (**avedesignstudio.com**)

Contents

Introduction	1
1 │ What punctuation is (and was)	3
What is punctuation?	3
Why do we need it?	3
Some approaches	4
Punctuation marks	5
Terminology	6
2 │ Stop!	7
Meaning and uses of the stop	7
The stop in action	7
Stops used with numerals	8
Stops in references and internet addresses	8
Cut short: stops or not?	9
3 │ In between: marks that contain stops	11
Question and exclamation marks	11
Semicolon and colon	15
The ellipsis	18
4 │ The ubiquitous comma	20
Meaning and uses of the comma	20
Isolating commas: marking a phrase or clause	23
Listing commas	29
Other uses of commas	34
A balanced diet of commas	42

5 |	Must dash	43
	Hyphens	43
	En and em rules	46
	Minus sign	48
	Underscores	49
6 |	Quote, unquote	50
	Quotations	50
	Quotation marks	51
	Speech	53
7 |	Brackets (in parenthesis)	56
	The parenthesis or aside	56
	Apposition	58
	Parenthetical dashes	58
	Parentheses (curved brackets)	59
	Brackets [square brackets]	60
	Braces {curly brackets} and angle brackets	61
8 |	Other marks and spacing	62
	Spaces	66
9 |	Where now?	71
	Expensive punctuation	71
	Changing practice	71
10 |	Resources	73
11 |	Glossary	75

Introduction

All of us, even professional editors, have moments of doubt about punctuation. If you've ever read a sentence and felt that something was wrong with the commas, but you couldn't decide what, or if you are not sure how to punctuate what you have just written, this guide is for you.

Sometimes you have to re-read a sentence because the punctuation seems odd. Is the weirdness an acceptable form of punctuation, a maverick author or just a mistake? Sometimes you revise your own punctuation, but it still seems wrong and you can't see how to analyse the problem or how to solve it. Perhaps you are unsure of the conventions or perhaps you never knew there *were* any. Like grammar, punctuation is based on the daily practice of millions of people, guided to some extent by experts who have studied it and identified best practice. It rests on conventions rather than rules. That is because language is too complex for simple rules, and context can overrule everything else.

This guide complements CIEP training, particularly the online course **Getting to Grips with Grammar and Punctuation**. The guide aims to answer four questions:

- What punctuation marks are used in British English text?
- What are the conventions in using these punctuation marks?
- Are there other ways to use some of these marks?
- What is the logic behind best practice and other usages?

This guide is based on reason: there should be a reason behind all our punctuation choices, a reason that makes sense to the reader. We hope you will enjoy the guide while discovering many things that you always wanted to know about punctuation but were afraid to ask.

✘ Examples in this guide showing faulty punctuation are marked by a red cross. Make sure you read the text around them: they are not models to be followed!

1 | What punctuation is (and was)

What is punctuation?

> The use of symbols such as full stops or periods, commas, or question marks to divide written words into sentences and clauses.

Collins Dictionary (2021)

Symbols, **sentences** and **clauses** are the nuts and bolts of punctuation and grammar, but the point of punctuation is to help us make sense of the text by preventing error and uncertainty.

> The practice, action, or system of inserting points or other small marks into texts, in order to aid interpretation; division of text into sentences, clauses, etc, by means of such marks.

Oxford English Dictionary (2021)

In conversation we can say 'I don't follow you' but in text we can't do that, so readers need signposts and waymarks to save them from getting lost. Punctuation is there to mark either a break or a change of direction.

Why do we need it?

We usually know what we mean to say, more or less, but people can still misinterpret it. In digital or printed text, with no facial clues, the likelihood of being misunderstood is even greater. As a well-known rule says, if it's possible to get it wrong, sooner or later somebody will get it wrong. If we want to communicate successfully, we need clear text with good punctuation.

Let her walk over my dead body.

Let her walk? Over my dead body!

Punctuation (from Latin *punctus*, 'point') began.with.points.between. words.to.help.when.reading.aloud becausepreviouslytherewereno capitalsgapsormarkstohelpthepoorreader.

Points between words were then replaced by spaces, and spacing too is a form of punctuation. As well as spaces between words, we use line spacing, **leading** (said 'ledding') and **indentation** to convey ideas to the reader.

Some approaches

Writing, like life, is full of decisions, and rules make decisions simpler. Many people like to have a rule to follow, so they prefer a prescriptive approach, prescribing the rules that must be followed and proscribing mistakes to avoid. Examples of this approach are the use of **serial (Oxford) commas** (see chapter 4) and hyphenating 'co-opt', though even the most prescriptive person will recognise that there will be exceptions.

By contrast, a lot of text can be unconventional in its use or non-use of punctuation, for instance in some fiction and in messaging, advertising or cartoons, where context and layout minimise the need for punctuation. Of course, an individual may punctuate prescriptively in one situation and much more lightly in another.

Punctuation can be expressive. Even people who see it as mostly pedantry may employ punctuation expressively, for instance by enthusiastic use of exclamation and question marks, often in multiple – and a final comment after a parenthetical dash can come across as a throwaway line.

Since the 1960s there has been a move towards minimal punctuation, driven by a desire for clean design and uncluttered pages, the main change being fewer commas. Too much punctuation slows readers down, though lack of it can also waste people's time by forcing them to go back and re-read.

The dictionary definitions get to the heart of punctuation: its basis is grammatical. Thus good punctuation should signpost the sense and reflect the grammar. Punctuation has conventions, but like grammatical rules they are subtle and adaptable.

Effective punctuation is an amalgam of general practice (what most readers will recognise and understand) and best practice (what most professionals recommend and can justify).

Punctuation marks

As a writer, editor or proofreader, you should be able to recognise and deal appropriately with about 30 different punctuation marks. It is your job to ensure clarity and consistency in the text, so you need to be clear in your own mind what each punctuation mark means and how it can be used. When talking about punctuation, you need to be aware that many punctuation marks have alternative names and multiple uses, depending on the style or convention being followed.

Most punctuation marks fall into one of five groups:

- points (stop, ellipsis, question mark, exclamation mark, comma, colon, semicolon and bullet)
- dashes (hyphen, en rule and em rule)
- strokes (solidus, prime and apostrophe)
- enclosures (parentheses, brackets, curly braces and various quotation marks)
- spacing (various kinds of spaces and indents, and leading).

We can use these marks in various ways but our punctuation should always clarify the sense.

Terminology

This guide is based on British terminology and usage. However, where punctuation marks have another name, we include the alternative. Since many editors work in US English and it is globally the commonest type of English, we give US terminology in parenthesis – for example, 'question mark (US query)' – and mention divergences between British and US practice.

2 | Stop!

Meaning and uses of the stop

We would struggle to decode text with no spaces, but we might fail completely without the stop. It has various functions, but it is always the end of something. The stop can be used:

- to mark the end of a completed sentence
- to bring a clause or phrase to an abrupt halt in mid-sentence
- after a number or letter that marks the place in a hierarchy or series
- to mark the break before the first decimal place
- to mark an abbreviation or other short form
- in a reference citation or internet address.

The stop also forms part of the question mark, exclamation mark, colon, semicolon and ellipsis. These marks are related to but distinctly different from the stop, so they are dealt with separately.

The stop in action

Commonly called the full stop, more simply the stop, this tiny mark is also known as the full point (traditional British) or period (mainly US); in internet addresses it is read and named as 'dot'. It typically marks the end of a completed sentence, which may be complex or simple. These are both completed sentences:

> Few of us speak in complete sentences, but that is the way we are expected to write.
>
> Stop.

A completed sentence has a **subject** (the actor) and a main verb. In the examples, the subjects are 'few of us' and 'you' (unspoken but understood in the second example); the main verbs are 'speak' and 'stop'.

Stops used with numerals

In any kind of publication we may see stops used in lists, after an initial number or letter, and similarly in other series or hierarchies, such as between number and title:

1. in volume, part, chapter or section heads
2. in numbered subheads
3. in figure, map or table captions.

A stop is also used in English-language publishing as a decimal point. In the past this point would have been in the medial position – level with the top of 'on', for example. In continental Europe the break before the first decimal place is shown by a comma.

Stops in references and internet addresses

References cram a lot of information into a small space, so the elements must be clear. Stops can be used in some styles between title and subtitle or between other elements.

> Carnevale, A., Schmidt, P. and Strohl, J. (2020). *The Merit Myth. How our colleges favor the rich and divide America*. Washington D.C.: The New Press.
>
> Danziger Isakov L, Kumar D, The AST Infectious Disease Community of Practice. Vaccination in solid organ transplantation. *Am J Transplant* 2013; 13 (Suppl 4): 311–17.
>
> O'Connor P., O'Hagan C. et al. (2019), 'Mentoring and sponsorship in higher education institutions: men's invisible advantage in STEM?', *Higher Education Research and Development*, vol. 39, no. 4, pp. 764–77, available at https://doi.org/10.1080/07294360.2019.1686468, accessed 16 September 2020.

Notice how differently these citations use stops; house styles make their own rules. Internet addresses – URLs, DOIs and email – use stops as part of their electronic identity. Some citations above use stops for abbreviations, but not all. Let's see why.

Cut short: stops or not?

One of the commonest uses of the stop is to mark the end of an abbreviation – or it used to be. Short forms are now everywhere in text because they help us deal with information overload, but if all of them were given final stops the effect might seem unsightly or overwhelming. For example, the 1964 *Concise Oxford Dictionary* listed R.S.P.C.A. and N.A.T.O. among its abbreviations but we would not write them like that today. In pursuit of clean design, the post-1960s consensus in British publishing has been that each of the four main kinds of short form has its own simplified conventions:

- Abbreviations (words cut short, such as v. for versus) generally need a final stop, which marks the amputated letters and tells us that we cannot read it as a whole word. However, abbreviations are now so common that readers have less need of this help, and the convention is often ignored.
- Initialisms (abbreviations in all caps or small caps, such as RSPCA, BCE) do not need stops, because the capitals show us instantly that they are short forms. We do not read initialisms as words.
- Acronyms (names/words based on initialisms, such as Unesco, scuba) do not need stops since we do read them as words; if they are names, we use an initial capital.
- Contractions (where the middle of the word is omitted, such as Dr, Ltd) do not need a final stop, the logic being that the end of the word is intact. These short forms tend to be well recognised.

Many of us are so used to these conventions that we hardly notice them. Like the rules of grammar, they have evolved as a result of widespread usage, encouraged by the irruption into public consciousness of longer and longer scientific names. DNA is clearly easier and quicker to read than 'deoxyribonucleic acid'!

We see differences in usage, because editorial practice varies and continues to change, albeit gradually. For example, St is sometimes used for Saint and St. (with a stop) for Street. Days of the week and months are often cut to three letters with no stop (eg Thu, Jan) and final stops are now often omitted from a.m./p.m. (standing for *ante meridiem/post meridiem*, Latin for 'before/after midday') or from authors' initials and postnominals. These trends can be expected to continue and go further.

Stops are less likely to be omitted in US English, which generally uses them in contractions and initialisms as well as abbreviations, as in 'the U.S. Government in Washington D.C.' or 'eds.' where British practice would omit all the stops.

An obscure fact

In some typefaces, italic and roman full stops are visibly different. Try it for yourself with stops side by side, using various fonts in Word. You may need to use the zoom tool to magnify them to 400%, although experienced proofreaders will often spot them even at 100%.

3 | In between: marks that contain stops

There are five punctuation marks that contain stops:

- question mark
- exclamation mark
- colon
- semicolon
- ellipsis mark.

Despite the stops they contain, all of these marks can be used in mid-sentence.

Question and exclamation marks

Both these marks can be used to end a sentence. When reporting speech (or within parentheses) they can also appear in the middle of a sentence:

> I may have said 'Oh?' or something. ... I had scarcely said to myself 'What ho, a banger!' when I saw who this banger was.
>
> PG Wodehouse, *The Code of the Woosters*

We may need to analyse what is really going on before we decide whether to use a question mark or an exclamation mark, and we may occasionally use both. Some questions are rhetorical – intended for effect, not expecting an answer – and some are exclamations phrased as questions:

> Do you have to? Isn't that just typical! Whose bright idea was this?!

More questionable questions

It may seem obvious that a question mark (US query) is used to end a question, but is it? We may not need a question mark in:

- questions that aren't really questions
- thoughts (wonderments) or musings
- some dialogue forms
- rhetorical questions
- questions that are really exclamations.

Questions that aren't really questions

If a question is posed as a statement, no question mark is needed, though one is often included. If dialogue includes a sentence that is a question only in form, the question mark may be omitted.

> 'Shall I tell her you called. It's Mr—?'

Julian Symons, The Colour of Murder

Some questions aren't really questions at all – or are they?

> How do you do? How are you? Can I help you? Lovely weather, isn't it?

All these examples expect some response, from mere acknowledgement (eye contact or a nod) to a substantive reply; in the last case, that could range from 'Yes' to a lengthy discussion of recent weather. Context usually tells us how genuine the question is, but choosing the best punctuation in each case is a recurring dilemma in fiction. If it looks like a question but the speaker does not seem to be looking for an answer, will readers be more distracted by a question mark or by its absence? We have to decide each case on its merits.

Thoughts (wonderments) or musings

Indirect questions (wonderments) are not phrased as a question but they imply one. They often use words like *surely*, *wonder* or *perhaps*. Indirect questions do not have a question mark at the end.

> I wonder which way is the exit. Perhaps that old lady might know.

If the wonderment is cast as a question, it usually needs a question mark. If it is embedded in a statement, there is no question mark. Musings can be presented either way.

> What's she trying to do? he wondered.
>
> He wondered what she was trying to do.

The question mark punctuates the end of the question clause, so no comma is needed after that (see *New Hart's Rules* 4.8.1, which warns against double punctuation), and the sentence continues with 'he' in lower case.

Some dialogue forms

Thoughts can also be punctuated with commas, like dialogue:

> The question is, what do I do now?

The comma after 'is' mimics the way we punctuate the start of an utterance in dialogue. We look at punctuation of dialogue under '**Quotation marks**' in chapter 6.

> He was wearing a cauliflower on his head. I asked myself why.

We could put 'why' in quotes with a question mark, but why give readers more characters to scan? They will understand that this is a thought, and they can easily complete it as 'why he would do that'.

A sentence containing a series of questions may be punctuated in various ways. Here are three:

> Have you ever seen an auk, or heard one or eaten one?
>
> Have you ever seen an auk, or heard one? – or eaten one?
>
> Have you ever seen an auk? Or heard one? Or eaten one?

Rhetorical questions

Like irony and sarcasm, rhetorical questions often do not mean what they say, yet they assume that the audience knows the answer. King Henry II made this mistake, with fatal results:

> Who will rid me of this turbulent priest?

When a speaker asks 'Who knows?' they seldom expect the answer to be '*I* know!' Nonetheless the questioning element is real. However, if the rhetorical question also has to spell out the scenario, it becomes complex and we may end up with a statement at the end of the question.

> Who knows whether, had it not been for Brexit, David Cameron might never have resigned?

This punctuation is awkward. It is better to put the question mark next to the question.

> Had it not been for Brexit, David Cameron might never have resigned. Who knows?

In more formal writing, a question mark (usually in parentheses) can indicate irony or sarcasm.

> Her friends (?) all agreed with her.

Questions that are really exclamations

There is some overlap in the functions of question and exclamation marks:

> What the dickens—? What the heck—!

Exclamations

The exclamation mark (US exclamation point) does what it says. These are typical uses:

> Hey, you! Ouch! Good heavens! Help!

It can be used to denote a shout, shock, surprise or amusement. It is much more heavily used now than in the past, and this has had two results: when used in multiple or repeatedly, it quickly becomes tiresome and loses its effect. If absent, it can make a personal message seem austere or unfriendly. Like a question mark, an exclamation mark that appears in mid-sentence is usually placed in parentheses.

> The main features of Paradise Row were the rubbish tip (!) and the nature reserve (and you would not believe how much rubbish there was in the nature reserve!) where we used to picnic.

Exclamation marks also have specific functions in mathematics and computer programming.

Semicolon and colon

A semicolon or colon is used to end a clause or **phrase**. Complex sentences often benefit from both semicolons and colons. Why do we need both? What's the difference? What do we use them for?

The semicolon

A semicolon is a full stop over a comma, indicating a halt but not the final stop; we mainly use it between (usually two) **independent clauses** to show that they are distinct yet linked, holding them in balance. Often the semicolon nudges us to compare the clauses, contrast them or find unexpected parallels.

> Pay no attention to what the critics say; no statue has ever been put up to a critic.
>
> Jean Sibelius, composer

> Marriage is a wonderful invention; but, then again, so is a bicycle repair kit.
>
> Billy Connolly, comedian

Some people have strong feelings about this modest little mark. Some love it, though writers who use it regularly are said to risk being labelled as intellectuals. It is possible to get through life without it and still write good prose, and people do, but a semicolon is subtle and nuanced: it implies comparison, contrast or balance, encouraging us to think critically about what we are reading.

As an intermediate level between stop and comma, semicolons can be used to clarify by:

- replacing commas in a run-on list where some list items themselves contain commas
- substituting for stops in a vertical list where at least one item contains a sentence or multiple clauses
- punctuating references
- articulating the structure of a long or complex sentence, as below.

> The purposes of higher education are preparation for employment; preparation for life as an active citizen in democratic society; the development and maintenance, through teaching, learning and research, of a broad, advanced knowledge base; and personal development.

A semicolon is needed for clarity before that last 'and', unless the last two **noun phrases** form one item. It can also be used to put a little more distance between clauses, as in this example.

> I never realised; but then I never asked.

It is not usual for a semicolon to introduce a list or an explanation.

An obscure mark?

An exclamation mark is known to printers and programmers as a bang – so, when combined with a question mark, the result was named the **interrobang** (Unicode 203D). A creature of the 1960s, it was meant to indicate astonishment or incredulity. Many typefaces do not include it, though it is seen occasionally in materials for teaching English as an additional language and in articles asking 'Why does no one use the interrobang?' They use ?! instead.

3 | In between: marks that contain stops

The colon

To quote *Hart's* 4.5, 'the colon points forward'. We use it in five main ways:

- to introduce a list
- to introduce a quotation or example
- before we exemplify or amplify the topic mentioned just before the colon
- before we show or explain the consequence of what has just been said
- in computer programs and after http or https in a website address.

The colon leads us to expect further enlightenment: more detail, more information or more insight. What comes after the colon must follow logically what went before.

If the list or quotation is set out, starting on a new line (displayed or extracted), we usually precede it with a colon, but we don't have to: we can use a full stop or, if a quotation runs on from the sentence, no punctuation at all. All three options also apply if the list, quotation, dialogue, explanation, conclusion (or whatever) is in the middle of running (body) text. There are no hard-and-fast rules in British English about how to punctuate a list; it depends on the client's house style or preferences.

A colon is also used in references (citations), typically to introduce page numbers (which some styles close up to the colon) or a subtitle, which some styles begin in lower case. In the following uses of the colon it is closed up (unspaced):

- between chapter and verse in references to the Torah, Bible or Qur'an (eg the biblical creation story is in Genesis 1:1–27)
- between hours, minutes and seconds in time of day or elapsed time (eg 07:30 GMT)
- to show proportion (eg head:body = 1:7).

In British English the first word after a colon usually starts in lower case (apart from names). However, some house styles specify an initial capital:

- Modern Languages Association (MLA), in all cases
- American Psychological Association (APA) and Associated Press (AP), if a complete sentence follows
- and possibly your client's house style (or your own).

The ellipsis

Ellipsis is the omission of words from a sentence. An ellipsis mark (usually just 'ellipsis') is a single character formed of three stops. It typically marks a place either where irrelevant matter has been left out of a quotation (in non-fiction) or where a sentence has been paused or left unfinished (in fiction). A quotation is, by definition, only part of what was said or written, so there is no need for an ellipsis at the start or end of it. If the ellipsis has been added by the editor, it is put in [square] brackets (see *Hart's* 9.3.3). The usual practice is to space off an ellipsis on both sides, using a **non-breaking space** before it. There is no space after it if a closing quote follows.

Completed sentences end in a stop. What about incomplete sentences? In dialogue they often tail off with an ellipsis and no further punctuation.

> 'I'm sorry ...' Leo began.
>
> Anthony Horowitz, *Killer Camera*

Leo's speech tails off, and the ellipsis marks the words left unspoken. Had Leo been interrupted, the break would be marked by an em rule. In both cases, the closing quote tells us that Leo has stopped speaking. If it was obvious who was speaking, the author might omit tags like 'Leo began'.

How do we punctuate ellipses in dialogue without *he said/she said/they said* tags? This is a question of style – author's, editor's or house – but it also depends on context. If the next bit of dialogue starts on a new line, as is usual, the preceding speech can tail off in an ellipsis followed by a closing quote and nothing. Tailing off into blank space reflects what is happening. If the ellipsis is followed by a new sentence on the same line, *Hart's* advises adding a stop before the new sentence. Space to taste.

3 | In between: marks that contain stops

At the time of writing, in texting and other informal contexts, even in emails, some people see a tailing-off ellipsis as loaded or ominous, so they use a dash instead (see '**Em rules**' in chapter 5).

4 | The ubiquitous comma

No punctuation mark is so useful nor so widely used as the humble comma, and no mark causes more doubt, disapproval and disagreement. Even if we do not overuse, underuse or misuse it, we are sure to be told that we have put it in the wrong place. Is there any truth about commas that we all agree on? Yes: we need commas.

Writers and editors get entangled in rules about commas, which tells us that the rules are not helping. Reasons are much better than rules, because reasons explain and justify decisions. There are some conventions, of course, and we will mention the most important ones. But we always need a reason to add or remove commas, and ambiguity is one good reason. Try deleting the comma before 'Gerard':

> I just don't understand, Gerard.

The comma prevents us reading 'Gerard' as the **direct object** of 'understand'. This is a good example of punctuation reflecting grammar, as it should. Unnecessary or badly placed commas are distracting and confusing, but commas are the first punctuation mark we turn to because they are versatile, effective and discreet.

Meaning and uses of the comma

Punctuation helps us make sense of the text, and commas do much of the work. Yet, with minor exceptions, the comma has really only two functions in prose.

- A comma can mark the beginning or end of a phrase or clause (an isolating comma).
- A comma can separate items in a list (a listing comma).

In the past these functions have been further divided and labelled – for example, two isolating commas used as a pair are often called bracketing commas – but all commas have one of the two functions listed above. And a listing comma is only isolating items in a list. A comma marks a small break or a change of focus, topic or (verb) subject.

> She carried the lamp to a workbench, where she cleared aside a saw, a paint-splattered shirt and a sheep's skull, until she found what she needed.
>
> Struan Murray, Orphans of the Tide

> It's simple. They like spicy food, and I don't.

> Most children eat crisps, even those whose parents believe in healthy living.

If the break is bigger, we need something with a dot: a stop, colon or semicolon.

There is also a third kind of comma. This is the one that is there simply because the writer feels that a comma is needed. We examine 'because we need one' commas at the **end of this chapter**.

In verse a comma is often used at a line end unless the sense runs on to the next line, but sometimes even if the sense runs on. Poetry doesn't follow rules!

> Around the couple,
> affection lingers,
> sweetening the air.
>
> David Bamford, 'Companionability', Rhymes and Reasons

Do I see a pause?

It is often said that commas mark pauses, but this is not a good 'rule'. Pauses are common in speech, but not all of them equate to a comma in writing, so we can end up with too many commas. A pause is the wrong place to start.

> ✘ On your marks, get ready, not yet, get steady, wait for it, go!

Those commas mark places where a speaker might pause, but the pauses are all different. Readers who haven't heard these phrases (starting a foot race) may be baffled. How would we punctuate them? Here is one possibility:

> On your marks, get ready— Not yet! Get steady. Wait for it ... Go!

In the past children were taught to add commas where they paused, which helped in reading aloud. We seldom read aloud, but silent readers need all the help they can get in decoding complex and unpredictable sentences at first go. Punctuation should match the grammar and the sense, unlike the next two examples.

> ✗ You did, what?

> ✗ He describes a toddler's view, relying on Piaget's idea, that cognitive development has stages.

Both writers have added a comma where they might pause, ignoring the grammar and trampling on the sense. The commas are forcing a break between things that go together grammatically: 'You did what?' and 'Piaget's idea that'.

Commas mark a break, albeit a small break. They do not join. (See '**The comma splice**'.) That is the job of conjunctions such as *or*, *and* and *although*.

> You must hand in your essay by Friday, or you will receive a mark of zero.

In that sentence, two clauses are separated by an isolating comma and joined by 'or'. The clauses have the same subject, 'you', so there is no grammatical reason for a comma. If this optional comma is justified, it is because there is a change of focus. That is why it can be helpful to add a comma before *but* when it introduces a **subordinate clause**, but there's no rule that says we must. US English users tend to expect a comma before the **coordinating conjunctions** *for*, *and*, *nor*, *but*, *or*, *yet* and *so*.

The only rule for commas that works in every situation is 'It depends'. Whether and where we add commas will depend on the grammar or the sense, or a complex balance of the two, but also on house style, writer's style (voice or habits), audience and context. Fiction may allow more flexibility.

Isolating commas: marking a phrase or clause

Sentence length alone is no reason for commas.

> A healthy male adult bore consumes each year one and a half times his own weight in other people's patience.
>
> John Updike, 'Confessions of a wild bore', *Assorted Prose*

Those 20 words contain one thought, fluently expressed. An apostrophe and a stop are all they need.

We might make sense of the two examples below even if they were unpunctuated, but the commas help us to decode them by presenting the sentence in chunks, isolating each thought and marking the places where the sentence changes topic or direction.

> Sadly, despite our advice not to use the shortcut, they got stuck in the ford, where they drowned.
>
> This is the house that Jack built, as he often boasts, although it was designed by Jill.

In the first example, a pair of commas isolate the aside 'despite our advice not to use the shortcut', and the third comma isolates the relative clause 'where they drowned', which again gives extra information. That comma also marks a dramatic turn in the narrative.

Introductory phrases

In any piece of writing, an editor's first decision on commas often comes in the first few words.

Despite appearances to the contrary, Mrs Ponsonby was not rich. Surprisingly, she was actually rather poor.

Are those isolating commas needed? No. Are they wrong? No. They will help some readers and irritate others. What would *you* do? As writer or editor, you may face the decision hundreds of times in any text because so many sentences start like this, with an **adverbial** followed by the main clause. Even if readers don't really need that comma, they still benefit by getting the sentence in chunks.

But too many commas will distract. An experienced editor will weigh these and other factors to make a rapid decision in most cases. One convention is to add a comma only if the opening phrase is five words or more. Some house styles have this rule; others forbid such commas.

Parenthetical commas (including bracketing commas)

A parenthesis is an aside, a group of words that can be cut and yet leave the sentence still making sense. It can be at the start of a sentence (like both of Mrs Ponsonby's above), in the middle (where it can be 'bracketed' by commas, like 'so to speak' in the example below) or at the end, as in Orwell's waspish final comment:

> The high-water mark, so to speak, of Socialist literature is W. H. Auden, a sort of gutless Kipling.
>
> George Orwell, *The Road to Wigan Pier*

The asides about Mrs Ponsonby flowed into the sentence at the start, with no break that needed a comma, but both of Orwell's parentheses definitely interrupt the sense, despite being only three and five words each.

How long can an unpunctuated aside be, and how many asides can there be in one sentence? The following sentence has asides of seven, four and eight words [shown in brackets] and a 12-word aside to an aside {shown in curly braces}:

[After a short tour of continental Europe,] Crozier was [on 8 March 1845] appointed to the *Terror* for Arctic exploration [at the express request of Sir John Franklin] {who was to lead the expedition to discover the north-west passage}.

Elizabeth Baigent, 'Crozier, Francis', *Oxford Dictionary of National Biography*

Only one comma in 40 words? Even that comma is not essential, but it *is* kind to readers. Often we need help to see where a parenthesis begins and ends or to see where a sentence is going.

Parenthetical commas are the simplest way to mark an aside, but they are not always the best choice. A reader seeing two commas near each other may wrongly assume that they are a pair of bracketing commas. Even if the commas are both parenthetical, they may belong to two different asides, so in a complex sentence we often need punctuation that differentiates. In this extract, pairs of brackets or dashes have replaced the previous commas and one comma has been added after 'staff':

The training of all professionals (doctors, nurses, co-ordinators and ICU staff, especially those involved in family interviews, formalities and discussions) is essential, and should include practical training – with simulated exercises such as breaking bad news, dealing with relatives' fears or grief and talking about dying, death and organ donation – as well as specific courses.

We don't need the comma after 'essential', and it could be removed.

Writers and readers can lose their way in long or complex sentences that use only commas or no punctuation at all. If in addition the subject of the sentence is stranded far from the main verb, they may not notice that the two do not agree in number and so they may lose track of the sense.

✗ A comprehensive **summary** of the various methodological approaches found in the most recent published studies – analysed with regard to the settings, participants, sample sizes, paradigms, systems of measurement and data characteristics – **are** shown in Table 1.

We have replaced commas with en rules here to isolate the aside 'analysed ... characteristics', making it easier to see that the verb should be 'is'.

We can easily trip over a short parenthesis that helps to identify location (eg county or US state), so it is usually marked by commas unless the state is just a two-letter abbreviation:

> The village of Loggerheads, Staffordshire, is named after its inn, the Three Loggerheads.
>
> Delaware University Press is based in Dover DE, Heinemann in Dover NH.
>
> Heinemann has offices in Dover, New Hampshire, and in Portsmouth, New Hampshire.

A parenthesis adding honours or posts held is usually marked by isolating commas and may also need listing commas. Postnominals are now generally punctuated only by spaces, as with US states in two letters:

> Anna Turner JP, Lord-Lieutenant of Shropshire, formerly High Sheriff, took up her post in 2019.
>
> Professor Hamish Scott MA PhD FBA FRSE MAE FRHistSoc is a fellow of Jesus College, Oxford.

Where parenthetical commas go wrong

A short parenthesis may not need commas but, if we add them, they must be in the right places. The test is: if we remove the text inside parenthetical commas, are we left with a complete sentence? Does it still make sense without the aside?

> ✗ Tariq reported a theft to me, and when I found Sam loading stolen goods into his car, I dismissed him.

The first comma should come after 'and' since 'Tariq reported a theft to me I dismissed him' is not a sentence; it doesn't make sense.

Apposition

> This insight, this understanding, led me to see that argument would not persuade him.

Apposition (like 'this understanding' above) is a special kind of parenthesis, usually delimited by commas. We can remove it without spoiling the sentence because the extra information it gives is a synonym for what came before. However, if adjacent commas are being used in other ways, this punctuation can be ambiguous, so always check whether the sentence could be misread.

> Among the close friends of Angela, Jan, Rani and Ben, there was no one who could juggle.

Do all four share the same friends, none of whom can juggle? If so, it needs rewriting to clarify this. Or is 'Jan, Rani and Ben' a phrase in apposition, listing Angela's close friends? If so, it might be wise to use parenthetical dashes or brackets to mark it.

When apposition is used to define relationship, punctuation can change the meaning.

> She was close to her sister Jane, but fell out with her brother, George, after his marriage.

The comma after 'brother' tells us that George = brother, so she had only one brother, named in apposition, whereas the lack of a comma after 'sister' tells us that Jane was not her only sister. If there is any risk of ambiguity, it is better to reword. If a name is in the possessive form, we do not need to add commas.

> Her mother Kate's cat disapproved of her sister Mary's dog.

Relative clauses (including defining clauses)

> The Sultan of Zanzibar was already regretting the war, which he had started half an hour earlier.

Relative clauses typically begin with a relative pronoun, such as *who, whom, whose* or *which*. Some clauses that begin with *that, where, when, why* or *what* behave in much the same way. Commas are very significant in such clauses. Recognise this?

> Sadly, despite our advice not to use the shortcut, they got stuck in the ford where they drowned.

Earlier we used this example with a comma after 'ford'. Without a comma, 'where they drowned' is now a **defining relative clause**, telling us which ford is meant. Very often a comma marks some inessential extra, and similar wording without a comma is defining.

> She looked scared, as if she knew what was coming.

> She looked as if she knew what was coming.

A comma can completely change the meaning, even with identical wording.

> Scientists who are often seen snoozing at work are not to be trusted.

Here the clause 'who are often seen snoozing at work' is essential to the sense: it defines the kind of scientists we are talking about, namely the snoozing ones. This is a defining (or restrictive) relative clause.

> Scientists, who are often seen snoozing at work, are not to be trusted.

In this version, with commas, the relative clause is disposable because it is parenthetical: it gives extra information about scientists, who all apparently keep falling asleep at work. It states: 'Scientists are not to be trusted'.

If a defining relative clause refers to a thing, British English allows a choice of relative pronoun:

> This is the house that Jack built. This is the house which Jack built.

Readers who use British English tend to prefer 'that' but don't mind 'which'; US English readers will tend to see 'which' as an error. Does it matter? It often does matter if the relative clause is defining, for example in giving directions.

> She lives in the first cottage that has a buddleia in the garden.
>
> She lives in the first cottage which has a buddleia in the garden.
>
> She lives in the first cottage, which has a buddleia in the garden.

The first version says: ignore all cottages until you find one with a buddleia bush. The third version says: go to the first cottage (it won't matter if you don't know what buddleia looks like). The second version creates doubt: does it mean the same as the first, or did the writer forget the comma?

Dialogue

Fiction allows more latitude in punctuation than non-fiction, though there are conventions. The biggest single punctuation problem in fiction is dialogue, in particular the placement of commas and quotation marks in relation to each other. We look at the position of commas in dialogue in '**Punctuation of speech**' in chapter 6.

Listing commas

Lists can be horizontal (within running text) or vertical (set out on separate lines, usually with bullets, arrows, numbers or letters); for vertical lists, see **chapter 8**. Commas are used to separate items in three kinds of horizontal (run-on) list:

- lists of nouns and noun phrases
- lists of adjectives or adverbs
- lists of verbs or clauses.

We look at each in turn.

Listing commas with nouns and noun phrases

The items may be nouns, noun phrases or *-ing* words used as nouns, also known as **gerunds**. For instance, Mr Toad's caravan contained (among other things)

> bedding, bookshelves, a birdcage with a bird in it, letter-paper, bacon, jam, cards and dominoes.
>
> Kenneth Grahame, The Wind in the Willows

We expect *and* between the last two items, though it is sometimes omitted in speech.

> I put in the stock, the goodwill, the shop, the tools – all the business in fact.
>
> Raymond Postgate, Somebody at the Door

Special care is needed if a list item itself contains *and* or *or*, like this message left by a parent:

> On your way home, could you get some milk, bread, butter, fish and chips?

What is the child to buy on their way home? If this is a list of five items, they will go to the supermarket and get some frozen fish and a bag of frozen chips, causing consternation when their parent comes home expecting a hot meal to be ready. If it is a list of four items, and they are to call at the chip shop, the last comma needs to be replaced (or supplemented, as here) by 'and':

> On your way home, could you get some milk, bread, butter, and fish and chips?

If the list (or a list item) is at all complex, or if an item includes commas, we usually turn to semicolons.

> Excise duties as of 1 June 2009 were HRK180.00 per 1,000 cigarettes in groups A, B and C; HRK38.00 per kg for tobacco; HRK1.10 per piece for cigars; and HRK4.40 per pack for cigarillos.

> I'm parking my toys: the big, red London bus; the battered dropside lorry with its load, if I can find it; the shiny black cab; and, best of all, the little, dark green sports car that Jo gave me.

We can also use brackets or dashes to mark parentheses within the list.

Listing commas with adjectives or adverbs

Commas between adjectives are now sometimes omitted. In the example above with its list of toys, should there be commas between adjectives? That depends on the writer, the context and the adjectives (or adverbs, eg *very*). If they all apply equally, we often add commas:

> A tall, dark, handsome stranger on a big, red bus – a very, very tall stranger.

If one adjective seems to be part of a fixed phrase (eg 'dropside lorry'), no comma is needed if we add just one adjective ('battered dropside lorry'). That also applies in the list of toys to 'black cab' if we see that as a concept or if we see 'shiny' as describing 'black'; but if the cab is equally shiny and black, a comma is added. This use of commas allows nuance in descriptions, especially in fiction.

In academic writing, there are often fixed phrases for recognised concepts. It is very important to be aware of current **terms of art** in the subject area that you are working on. Thus, if 'personal beliefs' is one concept, 'personal' is part of the noun phrase and one comma is sufficient in 'socially created, judgemental personal beliefs'.

Qualitative and classifying adjectives

One adjective – as in 'a tall stranger' – needs no comma. When we add another adjective, we create a list and we may have to stop and think. If we are fluent in English, we seldom need to think much because we know intuitively what punctuation to use and what order the adjectives go in. That usually depends on whether they are qualitative (also called gradable or coordinate) or classifying (also called cumulative) adjectives. A string of adjectives should sound natural, and what we are used to hearing largely fixes the order.

> A delicate little gilded blue porcelain jug

will sound more natural than

> A blue little porcelain gilded delicate jug.

Qualitative adjectives are usually separated by a comma, and

- are comparable (good, better, best)
- describe valuation, properties, age or colour in that order (fine, bigger, oldest, greenish)
- do not sound too odd if you swap them around (a fine, big house/a big, fine house)
- still make sense if you replace the commas by 'and' (a fine and big house).

Classifying adjectives are not usually separated by a comma, and

- come after qualitative adjectives
- describe origin, material or type in that order (German, silk, women's)
- sound odd if you swap them round (a German silk scarf/a silk German scarf)
- do not make sense if you insert 'and' between them (a German and silk scarf).

There are only two things to add. First, you need to be aware of these conventions, though you may rarely need to think about them if you follow them automatically. Second, the use of commas between adjectives or adverbs seems to be changing and may be on its way out, but make sure that your editorial decision is based on context (especially the likely audience) and be consistent within the document.

Listing commas with verbs or clauses

> Toad sat up on end once more, dried his eyes, sipped his tea and munched his toast.
>
> Kenneth Grahame, *The Wind in the Willows*

4 | The ubiquitous comma

> It was the best of times, it was the worst of times, it was the age of wisdom, it was the age of foolishness, it was the epoch of belief, it was the epoch of incredulity ...
>
> Charles Dickens, A Tale of Two Cities

Using commas we can make a list of clauses that refer back to the same subject, as Toad shows. It is unusual to do that as many times as Dickens does, but editorially it is not a problem. What is more unusual is to list clauses without 'and' between the final pair, as Dickens does here for effect.

If one independent clause is followed by another, we join them with a conjunction, usually *and*. If the second clause has a different subject, we normally add a comma before *and*, especially if there is some contrast between the clauses.

> The French are wiser than they seem, and the Spaniards seem wiser than they are.
>
> Francis Bacon, 'Of seeming wise', Essays

However, if the whole sentence is fairly short and simple, the comma may not be needed.

> They wreck the delicate instruments and the hero only just escapes with his life.
>
> Raymond Postgate, Somebody at the Door

Serial (Oxford) commas

The house styles of Oxford University Press (OUP), most US publishers and some others require a serial or Oxford comma. It is used in British English, but it is not the current norm. A serial comma is one before *and* or *or* at the end of a list, and it is always included ('consistently', to quote *New Hart's Rules*, the OUP style guide), regardless of context. For example:

> The flags of England, Ireland, and Scotland form the Union Jack's red, white, and blue.

Hart's 4.3.5 illustrates the serial comma with this example:

> cider, real ales, meat and vegetable pies, and sandwiches

Readers will assume that the comma after 'pies' is there to separate the sandwiches from 'meat and vegetable' – and *Hart's* confirms that is why it is there. So, even if the house style does not use serial commas, we may still need a comma in the serial comma position for disambiguation.

Yet in this case ambiguity remains: will we be offered two kinds of pie or 'meat-and-vegetable pies'? We could reorder to avoid the problem:

> cider, real ales, sandwiches and meat-and-vegetable pies

Some people feel very strongly about the serial comma, though it is hard to know how serious the novelist Philip Pullman was in writing that the Brexit commemorative coin 'should be boycotted by all literate people' because it lacks a serial comma. Some educators seem to insist on it, but opinions generally are divided about it. In any one publication, what matters is that the writer and editor are systematic in their use of commas because the reader relies on consistent punctuation.

Other uses of commas

Almost all commas are isolating or listing commas. Here we look at a few other uses of commas.

Job titles and aristocratic titles

If someone's job title is used as a noun phrase, it is normal to include *the*, with parenthetical commas around their name, as in 'The British prime minister, Boris Johnson, said ...'. In journalistic styles, the phrase is attributive and the statement becomes 'British prime minister Boris Johnson said ...'.

Similar questions arise when naming titled individuals. The most usual style is to put the title within parenthetical commas, as the *Oxford Dictionary of National Biography* does, in apposition:

William Capel, third earl of Essex, was married to Jane Hyde.

The comma splice

Punctuation interrupts. Commas interrupt, but gently. They do not join. If a sentence contains two independent clauses, we can't just splice them together with a comma.

✘ I love reading, I try to read a book every week.

✘ Few of us speak in complete sentences, that is the way we are expected to write.

It doesn't work. The reader, seeing a comma, assumes that the sentence continues, but soon finds that it has lost its way. What is coming next? A parenthesis? A list of clauses? In fact it is an independent clause. At that point we either add a conjunction like *and*, *but* or *though* to join to the independent clause that follows, or we insert a stop or semicolon to separate it.

Writers sometimes try to use *however* as a conjunction:

✘ Few of us speak in complete sentences, however that is the way we are expected to write.

But that 'however' is a linking adverb, not a conjunction, so we still have two independent clauses. In such cases we add a comma after 'however' to make clear that it does not mean 'in whichever way'. Here are three possible solutions:

Few of us speak in complete sentences, though that is the way we are expected to write.

Few of us speak in complete sentences; that is the way we are expected to write.

Few of us speak in complete sentences; however, that is the way we are expected to write.

However, the same structure – two independent clauses joined by a comma – can legitimately be used for effect, in **rhetoric** or in dialogue.

> I came, I saw, I conquered.
>
> He burst out 'I know, I know!'

The next example may look like a comma splice, but it isn't. The punctuation mirrors the grammar.

> The more he earned, the less he did.

Neither clause can stand alone and make sense, so in effect they are joint main clauses.

Commas 'because we need one'

Writers know what they mean, so they may not see any ambiguity or incoherence in what they write. They often add commas as random clues, but without any grammatical basis. This type of comma follows no obvious pattern and is very hard for readers to deal with. Editors try to clarify and anticipate misunderstandings.

> One person says, 'I need a comma to make the meaning of this sentence clear'; another finds the same sentence perfectly understandable without a comma.
>
> David Crystal, *Making a Point*

Punctuation is there to serve the reader. Beware of starting from the wrong end by listening for pauses and then sticking a comma in each one. Nonetheless, we may sometimes feel that a comma is needed, even though we find it hard to say why. For example, we might add a comma because what sounds natural in speech is baffling on the page.

> The question is, is it wrong?

Without the comma, the reader might at first assume that the repetition of 'is' must be a typo. If, in context, we see a good reason why a comma seems to be needed, by all means we should add it. One such situation is grammatical ellipsis.

Grammatical ellipsis and gapping commas

The word 'ellipsis' means simply omission. It usually refers to the ellipsis mark (see '**The ellipsis**' in chapter 3) but there is also grammatical ellipsis, which is common in English but may confuse less fluent readers. In the next example, the words in square brackets can be omitted and often would be.

> By that time I knew [that] the car thief was caught and the vehicle [was] safely retrieved.

That sentence does not need ellipsis marks because fluent readers will predict or assume the missing words.

If a writer prefers not to repeat a word, but feels the gap looks like an error, they may add gapping commas. In Trask's example, commas replace the missing words after 'France' and 'Poland':

> Italy is famous for her composers and musicians, France, for her chefs and philosophers, and Poland, for her mathematicians and logicians.
>
> Larry Trask, *Penguin Guide to Punctuation*

Grammatical ellipsis is so common in English that it seldom troubles fluent speakers or readers, and the sentence above is clear enough with just one comma, the one after 'musicians'. Trask demonstrates this convincingly by using the same text without gapping commas. Such commas are more justifiable if the 'repeated' word is in fact different ('are' for 'is' in this next example):

> War is, after all, the universal perversion and war stories, the pornography of war.

If we think readers may stumble over the gap and a comma will help, then we should add it. But most gapping commas are unnecessary and may just confuse or distract readers.

Sentence fragments

A form of ellipsis that is normal in speech, and thus common in fiction, is the sentence fragment. We can treat a series of fragments as a list, using listing commas, or we can treat each of them as a sentence.

> How would the white bear have behaved? Is he wild? Tame? Terrible? Rough? Smooth?
>
> Laurence Sterne, *Tristram Shandy*

Those six sentences include only two complete sentences. We understand the last four 'sentences' either as fragments of the previous sentence, completing a list that began with 'wild' (so we could use commas), or as fragments of their own sentences, each beginning with 'Is he ...'. Modern examples are often longer than that.

> These were the strangest weeks of my life. A life now forever changed because of what I learned.

The second part of that example is not a sentence, though it is punctuated as one. Grammatically it continues the previous sentence, and indeed it carries the sense forward, but it focuses on a new aspect of the same idea. A new aspect of the current topic is the characteristic of a new sentence, so it makes sense to present it as one. It is what we do in speech constantly.

Garden-path sentences

One good reason for a comma is to mark the start of a new clause with a different subject, especially if the lack of a comma would cause a garden-path sentence, one that leads the reader up the garden path until they reach a dead end and have to retrace their steps. Here are examples:

> All along Oak Avenue she saw friends and neighbours saw an interfering busybody.

> I like eating oranges and lemons are great for lemonade.

Both need a comma before 'and' to mark the start of a new clause.

In this next (real-life) example, who is using encryption? Is it the supplier, a criminal or an innocent customer? We can't tell.

> This is especially important to you as a supplier if the customer is a criminal who may be using encryption as a way to retrieve the evidence.

We need isolating commas, but there are two ways to make sense of it:

1. This is especially important to you as a supplier if the customer is a criminal, who may be using encryption as a way to retrieve the evidence.
2. This is especially important to you as a supplier, if the customer is a criminal who may be using encryption, as a way to retrieve the evidence.

In 1 the criminal is suspected of using encryption to retrieve evidence against themselves – with 'who ... evidence' as a non-defining relative clause. In 2 the supplier is retrieving evidence against the criminal – with 'if ... encryption' read as a parenthesis.

Commas with because *or* however

Butterfield's *Fowler* points out that *because* can cause genuine ambiguity that a comma can resolve.

1. I think he was angry because I heard him swearing.
2. I think he was angry, because I heard him swearing.

'Because', *Fowler's Dictionary of Modern English Usage*

In 1 he was angry at being overheard; in 2 his swearing is the evidence that he was angry. In the case of *however*, ambiguity is hard to imagine but a garden-path sentence is likely, and the presence or absence of a comma tells the reader which meaning the word has.

> However we pronounce it, controversy is controversial. *We* pronounce it correctly, however.

In the first case, the position of 'however' is fixed within the **dependent clause**. In the second case, 'however' can go at the beginning or end, or even (isolated by commas) in the middle.

Too many commas or too many words

In our enthusiasm to help the reader, we can overdo the commas. Gowers has a salutary example:

> It should be noted that the officer who ceased to pay insurance contributions before the date of commencement of his emergency service, remained uninsured for a period, varying between eighteen months and two-and-a-half years, from the date of his last contribution and would, therefore, be compulsorily insured if his emergency service commenced during that period.
>
> Ernest Gowers, *Plain Words*

We get five commas to trip over but no comma in the one place where it would help, where the sentence takes a new turn after 'contribution'. That is the only comma that is needed, so I join Gowers in suggesting just one comma in 55 words. Word count is only one factor. The text may not be simple, but it is clear with that one comma. Why burden the reader with more?

Yet we also said that it helps the reader if commas deliver the sentence in chunks, so which matters more? That depends on many factors, and the editor must judge between them, but context is all. As a rule of thumb when writing or editing, if you see one word between commas and it is not part of a list, look for a simple change that will remove a comma without altering the sense.

Commas in references

Note indicators in the main text (also called cues or markers, typically either superscript or in square brackets) may precede punctuation in some styles, but they normally follow punctuation in British English.

Each item in a reference list is itself a list, giving publication data in a fixed sequence. The data may be separated by stops, commas or colons, or very often by a mixture.

> Carnevale, A., Schmidt, P. and Strohl, J. (2020), *The Merit Myth. How our colleges favor the rich and divide America*, Washington DC: The New Press.

Styles that favour minimal punctuation may also use fewer capitals.

> Carnevale A, Schmidt P, Strohl J. *The merit myth: how our colleges favor the rich and divide America,* Washington DC: The New Press, 2020.

Commas used with numerals

Commas can also be used with numbers, in particular to make them easier to read:

- to separate numerals (in groups of three above 999, distinguishing them from years)
- to mark the first decimal place (common in many European countries, but not in British English)
- to separate numerals in chemical or biological labels (eg 1,3-didehydrobenzene).

In scientific, technical and mathematics work, digits may be closed up in numbers up to 9999 and a thin non-breaking space inserted after each group of three digits to the right or left of a decimal point, for example 10 100 or 3.141 593.

Italics with commas

If a piece of text in italics (such as a book title) includes commas, then the commas are inevitably italic; if a word or phrase in italics is followed by a comma that is part of the surrounding (**roman**) sentence, the comma is roman; if the sentence is italic, roman can be used as reverse italics.

A balanced diet of commas

There will always be tricky decisions about commas. Sometimes there are easy answers, for example if a comma has been missed in the middle of a list, or a non-defining relative clause has no comma before it or an aside in mid-sentence has a comma only at one end. Those conventions are well recognised. But, for people who like to follow rules, there is no set of rules (not even a good house style) that can resolve every dilemma.

There are three questions about commas that we often ask ourselves:

1. Does this need a comma? (If so, where should it go?)
2. Are there not enough commas here? (If so, where do I add one/them?)
3. Are there too many commas here? (If so, which do I remove?)

Whatever we decide, there should be a reason. We have looked at lots of situations where the first question arises, and the answers have suggested a balance between convention, convenience and reason. The second and third questions may seem hopelessly vague at first sight, but that is the clue: what do readers see at first sight? Do they see a jungle of commas and other marks, or do they see an unpunctuated desert? Before they read a word, they will have a first impression of a mass of text, and their brain will already have searched it for signposts and waymarks. How many they need, and what kind, will depend on the reader, content and context, so the writer or editor must continually judge what the reader needs.

The point of punctuation is to help readers, not necessarily to conform to rules.

5 | Must dash

Three types of dash are commonly used in text:

- hyphen (- the shortest),
- en rule (– usually twice as long as a hyphen) and
- em rule (— twice as long as an en rule).

All of them have more than one use in English-language publishing, and their usage varies according to the type of publisher or the audience, and the conventions used in the territory where the text is published. To complete our view of dashes, we also look briefly at the minus sign, underscore and text separators.

A hyphen can be used to link all sorts of words and even whole phrases:

> Ten-year-old Rani enjoys helping in a family-run garden centre started by her get-up-and-go great-grandfather.

An en rule, if used as a link, typically links two nouns. Note that, in some typefaces, such as Trebuchet, en rules look very like hyphens. If used as parenthetical dashes, en rules are spaced and em rules are closed up; hyphens are not used in this way. Butcher discourages mixing them, recommending '10- to 14-year-olds' rather than '10–14-year-olds'. US and British styles differ in their use of dashes, particularly em rules.

Hyphens

Hyphens look and act like staples: they fasten things together.

Hyphens help. They are seldom essential – just as, if you're a strong swimmer, a life-belt in rough seas isn't essential, but you might still be glad of it. Or was that a lifebelt? Hyphens can be optional.

Meaning and uses of hyphens

Hyphens show a close but unequal relationship between words, where one depends on the other. They are often a matter of house style or personal preference (eg 'post-war' or 'postwar') and their use may depend on context (the 21st century, but 21st-century blues). We can use hyphens in several ways:

- Attaching a prefix (eg pre-war, Co-op, Franco-Belgian, ex-MP, Trans-Siberian).
- Prefixing one noun with another to form an **attributive** (adjectival) phrase (eg music-hall star, life-size replica, two-thirds complete).
- Combining two words to represent one concept:
  » This is how compound words develop: a pair of words like 'web site' (where the noun 'web' describes the noun 'site') become bedfellows as 'web-site' (forming a noun or adjective) and then are mated as 'website'.
  » It is also the way double-barrelled names work: for example, the Bonham-Carters are the branch of the Carter family who inherited the estate of the Bonhams, so Bonham now describes Carter. Note that some double-barrelled surnames, like Vaughan Williams and Lloyd George, are unhyphenated.
- Attaching a suffix (eg credit-worthy, rumour-monger, not purple but purple-ish).
- Showing a **syntactic bond** in attributive phrases (eg a long-lost aunt, a suck-it-and-see approach, a well-known browser, connecting-rod bushes, common-sense methods) – and a hyphen tells us that a good-practice manual is not a practice manual that is good.
- Showing syntactic bonds of other kinds: adjective–adverb (eg left-handedly), verb–verb (eg shrink-wrap).
- Distinguishing meanings where the spelling is identical, which is sometimes a problem.
  » Was the group reformed or re-formed? Did the player resign or re-sign? Has the sofa been recovered or re-covered? Do you want a little-used car or a little, used car?
  » We can see (and hear) this same inequality in noun phrases derived from phrasal verbs (eg set-up, take-off, lay-by) where the verbs have no hyphen (to set up, take off, lie by).

- Showing a coinage or reduplication, or allowing words to lean on each other that cannot stand alone (eg flim-flam, topsy-turvy, higgledy-piggledy, hush-hush, riff-raff).
- Making it easier to read combinations of words with a single letter, a repeated letter or adjacent vowels (eg u-turn, X-ray, co-op, re-enter, re-admit, de-ice, over-run).
- In business, journalism and a few publishing houses, hyphens may be used for number spans instead of the more conventional en rule (eg pp. 34-5).
- In ephemera (flyers, tickets etc), hyphens may be used as parenthetical dashes.

We can often avoid hyphens by either running words together or keeping them separate. Some house styles include inconsistencies, such as 'lifebelt' and 'life-raft'. If the house style is silent, we may consult a dictionary or the *New Oxford Dictionary for Writers and Editors* while remembering that either is just one authority – albeit handy and widely recognised – and authorities can disagree. In editing or proofreading, always think about readability and consistency when deciding whether to hyphenate a word.

Hyphen decisions

Hyphens can be non-breaking, just like spaces. In MS Word Ctrl/Cmd + Shift + hyphen or Unicode 2011 produces a non-breaking hyphen, though it can look disconcertingly different on screen – often more like an en rule. If it is needed for readability – for example, where an entity that includes a hyphen is very short (as in 'the Bell X-1' or 'adverbs ending in -*ly*') – the editor should ensure that a non-breaking hyphen will be typeset.

Hard hyphens are added manually by the writer, editor or typesetter; soft hyphens are introduced automatically by word-processing software or a typesetting/layout program wherever a word may be broken by a line or page end. This task is best left to the typesetter. There is no single standard for programs that impose soft hyphens, though there are some common conventions. For example:

- No word should have two hyphens; so, if 'ex-soldier' straddles a line end, it must break at the hyphen.
- At least two characters should be left on each line.
- There should be no more than three consecutive line-end breaks.
- Words should be broken either into components (eg break-fast) or at doubled letters (eg bat-ted) in a way that will not mislead readers (eg he-arse). In British practice, word breaks tend to be based on etymology or pronunciation; the CIEP recommends the *New Oxford Spelling Dictionary*.

Hyphens in Chinese given names should not be cut: write Wang F-M or Wang Fu-Mei, not Wang F.

Many house styles hyphenate **adjectival phrases** if they are attributive ('a well-mannered child') but not if they are predicative, that is, acting as a **complement** ('She is well mannered'). Attributive phrases that include an adverb ending *-ly* are not usually hyphenated ('an awfully nice chap'), since the *-ly* ending makes its function clear.

Except at line ends, hyphens are normally closed up on both sides. However, in writing about 18th- and 19th-century history, pre- and post-war elections or ball-boys and -girls, hanging hyphens (suspended or dangling hyphens), which are non-breaking and spaced on one side only, are used. If clients prefer to avoid this, we will need to rephrase.

Styles have changed, and readers would now see 'to-day' and 'Oxford-street' as errors, though both forms were once common. If a client prefers 'web-site' to 'website', we would advise them that it will look odd or old-fashioned. But eliminating all hyphens is not a good idea either: how many and how old are 'three year old girls'? Hyphens easily distinguish 'three year-old girls' from 'three-year-old girls'.

En and em rules

The en rule and em rule (also called en dash and em dash) are both used as parenthetical dashes, so we begin with that use before considering other uses for the two marks separately.

Punctuating parentheses

Parentheses are asides, which may be clauses or phrases, long or short. They may be marked as separate (bracketed) by commas, dashes or curved brackets at each end. If they are short enough, they are usually left unmarked, like 'rather sharply' in this sentence:

> He said rather sharply that he didn't care.

If the aside is more noticeable than that, the next choice is usually commas, as shown by a line attributed to Dorothy Parker:

> Why, after all, should readers never be harrowed?

If the aside is an obvious digression or seems irrelevant – and this is something my Uncle Albert, now 76, once told me – then parenthetical dashes are usually best, especially if commas have already been used or if the digression comes at the end of the sentence. If the aside adds relevant, but incidental, facts then brackets (usually curved brackets, which editors call parentheses) mark its separateness (see '**Parentheses (curved brackets)**' in chapter 7).

Parenthetical dashes

British styles typically use spaced en rules as parenthetical dashes, though Oxford University Press and some others use unspaced em rules. Most US styles use unspaced em rules; US newspapers use yet another style, spaced em rules.

Used in pairs, parenthetical dashes mark an aside; used singly before the last part of the sentence, they mark an afterthought, punchline or conclusion. Dashes catch the eye – especially spaced en rules – and so create a larger break than commas. However, they are also more informal, so a final comment after a parenthetical dash may come across as a throwaway line. We look at parenthetical dashes again in **chapter 7**.

No other punctuation should adjoin spaced en rules, and no character should invade their space.

En rules

In MS Word on a PC you can produce an en rule with Ctrl + minus sign (on the numeric keyboard); on a Mac keyboard it is Alt/Opt + hyphen. It is also found under Insert Symbol.

When closed up, an en rule shows an equal relationship of:

- polarity (eg the Tyson–Holyfield fight, UK–US relations, the teacher–pupil relationship)
- congruence (eg the Mason–Dixon line, Epstein–Barr virus, an actor–manager)
- points at each end of a continuum (eg the Crewe–Euston line, pp1–7, ages 8–9).

Em rules

In MS Word on a PC you can produce an em rule with Ctrl + Alt + minus sign (on the numeric keyboard); on a Mac it is Shift + Alt/Opt + hyphen. It is also found under Insert Symbol.

An em rule is often used in fiction to end an incomplete sentence, especially where dialogue or reported speech is broken off or interrupted by another speaker or by an event (*Hart's* 4.11.2).

> 'What the—! Put that gun down before you—'

An incomplete sentence may be ended by an ellipsis if it just tails off (see 'The ellipsis' in chapter 3). An em rule is also sometimes used to mark omitted letters or words.

> 'Tell me, did Lady J— write to you? I haven't heard anything. I just thought ...'

Minus sign

The minus sign is not a punctuation mark, but it is easily mistaken for one. Some writers use a hyphen or an en rule for a minus sign, which editors should change to the distinct character available in MS Word via

Insert Symbol or Unicode 2212. A proper minus sign sticks to its number, even at a line end, and aligns with the horizontal line of a plus sign. An en rule is slightly lower.

Underscores

Some internet addresses include underscores and/or whitespace characters as a kind of punctuation, but they are not easily recognised by search engines and are best avoided. Where the style is to underline URLs, the underscore may not be visible; this does not matter if the link works, but it does matter if for any reason readers need to type out an internet address.

6 | Quote, unquote

Quotations

Shorter quotations are normally placed inside quotation marks and run on (integrated) within the text. Most house styles have rules for quotations longer than 25 to 60 words, or three to five lines, which are displayed (extracted); that is, they begin on a new line, are indented on one side or both, with a space above and below, and are not enclosed in quotation marks. Ellipses are used to indicate missing material within the quotation, but not at the beginning or end (see '**The ellipsis**' in chapter 3).

Punctuation of quoted matter

In serious non-fiction, people and publications must be quoted with strict accuracy; this is essential to authorial and editorial ethics alike. *Hart's*, which is aimed primarily at editors of serious or scholarly works, advises in section 9.3 that 'punctuation should normally follow the original ... Forms of punctuation that differ from house style may be silently regularized'. How do we square this circle?

Scholars and academic presses may well reject any editing of quoted matter, and of course authors and editors owe a duty of care to quoted sources: they have authors too. Nonetheless, changing double spaces to single, unspaced em rules to spaced en rules or double quotes to single (or the reverse, in all cases) and removing stops from some abbreviations are matters of style, not substance, and are usually uncontroversial. Changes to spellings and adding or subtracting commas or hyphens go further: they subtly disguise the voice of the person being quoted. These are usually a step too far, though context is the final arbiter.

Readers expect quotations to be attributed, either in the running text – for example, 'As Dickens says in *Hard Times*' – or in parentheses, which may follow the quotation or be placed (less distractingly, some would say) at the end of the sentence (*Hart's* 9.2.5). These conventions apply equally to integrated and displayed quotations. *Hart's* has good advice for any editor, fiction or non-fiction, but quotation and speech present different dilemmas, so we look further at punctuating dialogue in the section on '**Speech**' below.

Quotation marks

If we quote verbatim what someone said or wrote, we put it in quotation marks, also called quotes, speech marks or inverted commas. These can be 'straight' (vertical) or 'curly' (smart) and 'single' or "double" (often called [66] and [99] by children). Straight quotes are a hangover from typewriters, but now usually betray cut-and-paste text from an email or website, where straight quotes are the norm. Curly quotes are angled and have different shapes (very like [6] and [9]) for opening and closing quotes – in most typefaces, that is, but not in this one, which is Open Sans. Other languages have their own marks, some of them similar to English, some (like French «guillemets») quite different.

Single or double?

US practice is usually double quotation marks first, whereas in British convention it is a matter of house style: double quotes are used (at least for quotation or dialogue) in newspapers and magazines, children's books and some other book publishing; elsewhere single quotes predominate. If quoted matter in double quotes includes a quotation, it is put inside single quotes; the style sheet will call this 'double quotes (single within)'. If the style is single quotes, the style sheet will say 'single quotes (double within)'. If the quotation within the quoted matter itself includes a quotation, as can happen in dialogue, the style alternates again.

It is also possible (depending on house style, of course) to use single and double quotes for different purposes: for example, double quotes for quotation and dialogue, with single quotes for everything else. We look next at what 'everything else' can include.

Uses of quotation marks

Most readers are accustomed to seeing quotation marks used for the following text elements:

- *quotation
  » from a published work or interview
  » from a letter, email or forum post
  » from a conversation
- dialogue (reported speech)
  » thought or monologue
  » quoting someone else
- a nickname, pseudonym or codename
- *a current, common or colloquial expression
- dialect or slang
- *the term or topic under discussion
- *a term of art, jargon or special term (eg the 'thingness' of things) on first, defining, mention
- a term that might not be recognised as such (eg 'i')
- a translation or gloss of a foreign word or term
- a proverb, maxim or motto
- *the writer's distancing from a term (scare quotes)
  » ironic or satiric (eg NHS 'reform')
  » so called (eg the 'Free Republic of Liberland')
  » unspeakable (eg swear words, terms of abuse)
- titles of minor published works (usually roman with **minimal capitals**)
  » chapters of a book, articles in a newspaper or journal
  » tracts, booklets, pamphlets, shorter poems
  » dissertations, unpublished works
  » prints, sketches, cartoons
  » short pieces of music, hymns, songs, first lines of poems or lyrics
  » broadcast episodes (eg 'The man and the hour' from *Dad's Army*).

In many cases the reader will have no doubt about the reason for using quotes, but inevitably there are also situations where they may mistake the intended meaning or be quite uncertain. This is particularly likely with the usages that are *asterisked, especially if a single word is in quotes.

In the next example, do the quotes mark a quotation or a colloquialism? If the style uses single quotes for all purposes, we can't tell.

> This 'slip of a girl' from Yorkshire was just what Geoffrey de Havilland needed to assure the public that anyone ... could safely fly the reliable Moths that his company was producing.
>
> <div style="text-align:right">Robin Higham, 'Johnson, Amy', <i>Oxford Dictionary of National Biography</i></div>
>
> You can't drive if you are 'unfit through drugs', even if they are prescribed drugs.

In this advice to users, we can guess that *can't* means *can't legally*, so this is quoting the relevant Act of Parliament. Ask yourself: do quotes make any difference? The answer here is effectively none, so we are wasting the reader's time by making them wonder: why the quotes?

Speech

We noted above that double quotes are sometimes reserved for quotation or dialogue, with single quotes then being used for other purposes. Dealing with quotation is fairly straightforward, as long as we are scrupulous about accuracy and attribution, though using single or double quotes for everything can sometimes be genuinely ambiguous.

Editing dialogue brings different problems. In chapter 3 we considered the punctuation of **questions, wonderments and exclamations**, and in chapter 4 we touched briefly on dialogue. Here we discuss the perennial question in punctuating speech: the placement of quotation marks.

Punctuation of speech

Problems do arise in reporting or transcribing speech, mostly because of speech tags (dialogue tags). In speech on the page, a comma separates the remarks from the name of the person addressed, and the comma before 'Gerard' is one of these vocative commas.

> 'I just don't understand, Gerard,' she said. 'Actually I don't think anyone else does either.'

The comma after 'Gerard' separates speech from reporting, but it also represents a full stop in the narrator's speech. If the writer can manage dialogue without speech tags, the punctuation is simpler (here shown using the double quotes option).

> "Twelve years old now and you still don't do chores! What sort of a son are you?"
>
> "The sort you wanted. After all, you brought me up, Mum."

Let's add speech tags after the first four words. British books used to do this differently, but US practice, which is now general in almost all British fiction publishing (see *Hart's* 9.2.3), puts commas inside the quotes:

> "Twelve years old now," she said, "and you still don't do chores! What sort of a son are you?"
>
> "The sort you wanted," he shot back. "After all, you brought me up, Mum."

Finally, at the end of a sentence Chicago (US) style places the stop inside the quotes, and a colon or semicolon outside, in both fiction and non-fiction. British practice places the closing quote after the stop if the last word in the speech completes a sentence, as in the first line below; if the speech is a sentence fragment, the closing quote comes before the stop.

> Ronnie had an idea: 'Give a supper party on the first night! That's what I'd do.' When someone asked what Ronnie did, the answer was that he had 'friends who have independent incomes'.
>
> adapted from Saki [HH Munro], *When William Came*

As for queries, ask yourself: have I attached the question mark to the question or to the wonderment?

> How often does someone tell you they don't want a cup of tea and you come away thinking 'I bet they really did want a cup of tea'?

Non-fiction variations

Placement of commas and stops inside quotes, independent of sense, with colons and semicolons outside, is the norm in US non-fiction, as in the next two examples:

> As Farrington said, "Simplified English will not compensate for a lack of writing skills."
>
> John R. Kohl, *The Global English Style Guide* (2008)

> Milligan complained that "they didn't even read my piece in 'Pseud's Corner.' Bit rude, I thought," but he never mentioned the matter again.

However, academic studies that require more precision follow 'the exacting British system' (*The Chicago Manual of Style*, 17th edn (2017), 6.9) where anything within quotation marks must match the original.

> Milligan complained that 'they didn't even read my piece in "Pseud's Corner". Bit rude, I thought', but he never mentioned the matter again.

This is also the practice followed by those people posting on social media or forums who use 'logical punctuation' or 'logical quotation'. Wikipedia's principle of minimal change is similar.[1]

Careful punctuation helps readers by clarifying what was said or thought, or quoted.

---

[1] english.stackexchange.com/questions/221689/is-the-logical-system-of-punctuation-becoming-more-prevalent-in-the-us.

7 | Brackets (in parenthesis)

In this chapter we examine the several kinds of bracket, including parentheses, and we look again at ways of punctuating a parenthesis. The first meaning of the word 'parenthesis' is an aside, as seen in pantomimes like *Jack and the Beanstalk*:

Jack (glumly): This cow's not worth a bean.

Cow (aside): Oh, yes, I am.

Dealer (aside): Oh, no, you're not.

adapted from Val Neubecker, *Jack and the Beanstalk Rap*

The other meaning of 'parenthesis' is a punctuation mark, one of a pair of curved brackets (parentheses) that we can use to mark the start and end of an aside.

Writing, when properly managed (as you may be sure I think mine is), is but a different name for conversation.

Laurence Sterne, *Tristram Shandy*

The parenthesis or aside

We have looked at asides already, first in '**Parenthetical commas**', chapter 4, and then in '**En and em rules**', chapter 5, where we noted four approaches to punctuating parentheses: nothing, commas, dashes and curved brackets.

Nowadays we can see as never before that the peril which threatens all of us comes not from nature, but from man.

CG Jung, *Memories, Dreams, Reflections*

7 | Brackets (in parenthesis)

Englishmen don't shake hands all the time like Americans and although he wasn't English he had some of the mannerisms.

Raymond Chandler, *The Long Goodbye*

These two examples show parentheses with no punctuation: 'as never before' is short enough that the reader can absorb it without help. With an unpunctuated aside much longer than that, the reader may start to lose their way. In a longish sentence 'although he wasn't English' is tolerable if noticeable, but context matters: that non-stop delivery is one of Chandler's recurring devices.

Before the war, and especially before the Boer war, it was summer all the year round.

George Orwell, *Coming Up for Air*

Commas are the default for asides, being easy to follow and unintrusive. Try the Orwell quote with dashes, then curved brackets and then nothing. It would still be comprehensible with no internal punctuation, but the lack of guidance might cause readers to slow or stumble and perhaps miss the sly shift from Great War to Boer War; dashes or curved brackets would call too much attention to the aside.

He went to Dr Bunch – he's been going to him for years – and complained about his ribs, and told him they seemed to be giving him claustrophobia.

NF Simpson, *The Hole*

The Simpson quote is different because the aside is an independent clause, which needs either to be joined (by a conjunction or relative pronoun) or properly separated (which a comma cannot do). The options there are parenthetical dashes or curved brackets. We saw curved brackets being used by Sterne above.

I've written a riposte to that book [*Eats, Shoots and Leaves*] already (*The Fight for English*, 2006), so I won't repeat the arguments here.

David Crystal, *Making a Point*

More often, curved brackets (parentheses) are used to cite a source, as David Crystal does here; the title of Lynne Truss's book is our interpolation in [editorial] brackets.

Apposition

We discussed apposition earlier (in **chapter 4**), but here we note that it can be marked by commas, brackets or parentheses, or by all three for different purposes.

> Anne Clifford [known as Lady Anne Clifford], countess of Pembroke (1590–1676), was born on 30 January 1590, the only surviving child of George Clifford, third earl of Cumberland, and his wife, Lady Margaret Russell.
>
> adapted from Richard T Spence, 'Clifford, Anne', *Oxford Dictionary of National Biography*

Occasionally a phrase in apposition may be marked by parenthetical dashes, as an aside can be. We hasten to add that this line from Shaw's play was not meant to be taken seriously, even then:

> Bulgarians of really good standing – people in our position – wash their hands nearly every day.
>
> GB Shaw, *Arms and the Man*

Parenthetical dashes

We mentioned in '**The parenthesis or aside**' above that parenthetical dashes are appropriate in a long, complex sentence with multiple asides or dependent clauses –

> We got it all planned before he was born that if we had a white baby we were going to dress him in black – or her in black if we had a girl – and if either of them were black we'd have everything white, so as to make a contrast.
>
> NF Simpson, *One Way Pendulum*

– but they can also give a casual look, since a dash is the easiest punctuation mark to dash off.

> Yes – oh dear, yes – the novel tells a story.
> EM Forster, *Aspects of the Novel*

At the end of a sentence, a parenthesis can act as a throwaway line, especially after a dash.

> It's only eighty miles as the crow flies – and our crow is a sick man.
> Spike Milligan and Eric Sykes, 'The siege of Fort Night', *The Goon Show*

A parenthetical dash after the opening of a sentence is rare and rather unorthodox.

> She's shy – of the Violet persuasion, but that's not a bad thing in a young girl.
> Ronald Firbank, *The Flower beneath the Foot*

Parentheses (curved brackets)

Curved brackets, which editors call parentheses and other people call round brackets, or simply brackets, put more distance than commas or dashes between the aside and the surrounding text. We tend to use them for relevant information that is incidental or inessential, or that may be important to some readers but not others.

Parentheses are often used to establish abbreviations, and for measurement conversions, dates, reference citations, contributors' affiliations, cross-references, translations, synonyms and **glosses** (if there is no glossary).

> Withdrawal of life-support treatment (WLST) must be delayed until a retrieval team is ready (if the family agrees). Each state has its own rules on evidence of prior consent (eg checking donor registries) and the vital signs (saturation, pulse and blood pressure). Another approach for kidney transplants is subhypothermic (27–32°C) regional perfusion (see chapter 5).
> adapted from EDQM, *Organs for Transplantation*, 7th edn

Mt Smrek (in Czech: Smrk) track is 10 km (6 ml) long; the maximum gradient is 5% (1 in 20).

Gavin Hamilton (1723–1798) excavated Roman sites at Ostia (1774–9) with great success.

adapted from Elizabeth Angelicoussis, *Reconstructing the Lansdowne Collection of Classical Marbles*

Curved brackets are also used to economically represent alternatives, such as the singular and/or plural form(s).

Brackets [square brackets]

Square brackets are generally used for editorial comment, expansion, explanation, identification or intervention in someone else's text, typically in a quotation or in a scholarly edition of a historic or literary text. Tristram Shandy calls them 'crooks' in his account of Uncle Toby's apologia.

> I have had the good fortune to meet with it amongst my father's papers, with here and there an insertion of his own, betwixt two crooks, thus [ ], and is endorsed, my brother Toby's justification of his own principles and conduct in wishing to continue the war.
>
> Laurence Sterne, *Tristram Shandy*

Brackets are used where a bibliography identifies an anonymous author.

> [RP Knight], *Specimens of Antient Sculpture*, I (London 1809).

A longer omission can be shown by an ellipsis in brackets, thus: [...].

> They came 'from a vineyard near the tomb of Mitellus [Caecilia Metella] on the Appian Way'. [...] Among the finds from Tivoli, 'Cincinnatus taken from the plough [Cat. no. 15], the same as that at Ver[s]ailles, [but] of better sculptour' was in fact a statue of Mercury.
>
> Elizabeth Angelicoussis, *Reconstructing the Lansdowne Collection of Classical Marbles*

Square brackets are sometimes used inside round brackets to avoid nesting round brackets. There are special uses for brackets in programming, mathematics, linguistics and other fields, but the only other use that most of us will find for them is to present text citations in Vancouver (numbered list) references, though this is also done with superscript numbers.

Braces {curly brackets} and angle brackets

Braces { } are seldom seen in text unless a third type of bracket is needed; however, they are used for specific purposes in music, linguistics, mathematics and (IT) programming.

Angle brackets < > have specific uses in computer programming. In copyediting they can be used to enclose style tags (typically for heading levels, paragraph styles and displayed elements) to be picked up by the typesetter or designer.

8 | Other marks and spacing

Special marks

The apostrophe

There are three conventional uses for the apostrophe:

- to indicate possession

  Jill's hat, the girls' coats

- to indicate omission

  'don't' for 'do not'

- to improve clarity or readability

  'There are two i's in Hawaii'

For plural owners ending -*s* (eg girls), the apostrophe goes after the -*s* (the girls' coats). In all other cases the apostrophe normally comes first (eg Jane's flat, James's pad, the men's room). Some styles omit -*s* where it would seem awkward after a classical or biblical name (eg Aeneas' travels, Jabez' name).

For do's and dont's we can instead write dos and don'ts – you decide which – but using apostrophes is a common style preference, such as when minding your p's and q's.

Apostrophes are now commonly dropped from company names (eg Selfridges, Barclays) and we no longer write *sha'n't* for *shall not*, or *'phone*, *'bus* and *'cello* for *telephone*, *omnibus* and *violoncello*. Against the trend, King's Cross station first adopted an apostrophe only in 1951 but still retains it.

Some special marks

Prime: '

Double prime: "

Solidus: /

Text separator examples: & ℯ ℛ ℐ ֍ ★ ✳ ✱

Pilcrow: ¶

Section sign: §

Prime and double prime

Prime (') and double prime (") are straight characters in the superscript position; they usually lean to the right. In some typefaces it can be difficult or impossible to distinguish a prime from an apostrophe or single quotation mark.

Single and double primes are used to show respectively feet and inches or minutes and seconds (of angle or time); they also have specialised uses in mathematics, chemistry, physics, linguistics and music. Unicode 2032 is prime and U+2033 is double prime.

In a dictionary entry, a prime can be used to mark (the end of) a stressed syllable.

In music, primes are used to show pitch. Middle C is c', the C above that is c", and so on. Plain c is the note an octave below middle C; the note two octaves below is upper-case C, and the note a further octave down is shown either as CC or as C with a subprime symbol (which seems to have no Unicode number).

The solidus

The solidus – also called a slash, a forward slash, an oblique or a stroke – is Unicode 002F and it has numerous uses. We list here the meanings that you are likely to meet in British English.

Most often a solidus means 'or' (eg yes/no, and/or). It has become useful as a way of presenting disputed or alternative names (eg Falklands/ Malvinas, Yr Wyddfa/Snowdon).

An oblique stroke can show ratio, meaning *'per'* in measurements (eg km/hr) or *'out of'* when giving a test mark or any position in a numerical sequence (eg 10/10 = full marks; page 14/16 = the 14th page of a 16-page document).

Among widely recognised abbreviations that developed informally, some use the solidus to separate words (c/o = care of, u/s = unserviceable, n/a = not available, w/e = week ending, and 24/7 = open day and night all week). In pre-decimal currency, a solidus was often used to divide shillings from pence (eg 2/6 = 2s. 6d.) and sometimes pounds from shillings (eg 1/15/0 = £1 15s. 0d.); a dash (hyphen or en rule) showed 'no pence' (eg 10/-).

Dates can be presented with strokes (DD/MM/YYYY in British practice, MM/DD/YYYY in US practice and YYYY/MM/DD in the ISO standard). This is often ambiguous (eg 9/11 = 9 November in the UK but September 11 in the US) so it is wiser to use three-letter forms like Nov or Sep. A stroke can also indicate a time period that does not match the usual divisions of days, months or years (eg the night of 24/25 December, in May/June, the financial or academic year 2021/22).

A solidus is used in linguistics before and after a pronunciation (eg quite / kwʌɪt/), and in poetry to mark a stressed syllable.

Where verse is quoted in running text (prose), solidi are used to mark line breaks.

> There was an old man in a tree / Who was horribly bored by a bee / When they said 'Does it buzz?' / He replied 'Yes, it does! / It's a regular brute of a bee.
>
> Edward Lear, *A Book of Nonsense*

Copyeditors and proofreaders know the solidus as mark A1 'end of change' in the BS 5261 standard proof-correction marks. It is not a vertical bar, as the Wikipedia article 'Slash' says; it is called an 'oblique' in mark B33, and the closing strokes in BS 5261 (eg marks B1, B19, D2) are at 80° – an angle that saves space and aids clarity. A solidus can also show negation in BS 5261 (eg marks B16, B17).

In mathematics, solidi can show negation as well as division or fractions, although slightly different characters called the fraction slash and division slash are now preferred. Because of their use in computer programming, solidi are familiar as separators punctuating webpage URLs.

Text separators

Any text, fiction or non-fiction, can include separators, also known as graphic dividers, fleurons, printer's flowers or horticultural dingbats. Some of them are found in the Dingbats symbol menus, but (the author may need to be warned that) they are not included in every font. Commonest are the tilde (swung dash) and hedera (ivy leaf). These little devices mark a change of focus or topic within a chapter or create a break like that of a subhead, but wordless. They can also be used to separate elements in a chapter opening or in running heads and footers. As long as they are in the right place, there is little to go wrong. Famous last words.

Pilcrow

The pilcrow symbol began life as the marker of a new paragraph, and it is still sometimes used when citing a paragraph in a legal document or in a manuscript or other unpaginated document. In word-processing software it is used to mark the end of a paragraph (using the Enter or Return key), though it may not always be displayed; a pilcrow also denotes the button that hides/shows pilcrows and other formatting.

Section sign

The double-s represents its name, *signum sectionis*. Depending on the document's nomenclature, the symbol can be referred to or read out as 'section', 'clause' or 'paragraph' (US also 'area' or 'segment') when denoting divisions in a statute, legal code, agreement or treaty.

Spaces

The point that once marked the end of a word was replaced by a space. Spaces have become an important form of punctuation – and not just between words. After paragraphs had been invented, they came to be marked by a line space or half-line space above and below – called leading – or by a first-line indent (a fixed space before the text begins).

As a special kind of paragraph, a displayed quotation (or extract) is usually given extra leading both above and below, together with a left indent – and often a (smaller) right indent as well. Extracts may also be distinguished by being set one point smaller or in italics, or in a different typeface. Headings are punctuated by a surround of white space, which helps the reader to navigate the text. The space above a heading needs to be large enough (a line space, typically, though it can be more) to clearly mark a break or change of direction.

In general, white space not only punctuates text but helps it (and the reader) to breathe. Interline spacing, suitable margins (the head, foot, fore-edge and gutter may all be different) and fresh rectos at chapter heads all make a difference. So does space around tables, figures, notes or lists, with hanging indents for turnover lines in headings (including captions) and lists.

Special spaces in text

In word-processing software, the spaces between words are not all the same unless you combine plain text with a fixed font, like Courier on a mechanical typewriter. In justified text on screen, a proportional font automatically adjusts the tiny amount of white space around each character to even out the spaces between words, stretching or squeezing lines to ensure they fill the text measure.

Standard spaces between words come in a variety of widths, and a thin space is needed often enough for BS 5261 to have a separate mark (D5) for it. Non-breaking spaces are available in several widths. A standard non-breaking, fixed or hard space (in HTML) may be used between the following (but only if that is the style preference):

- initials that form part of someone's name (eg J. R. R. Tolkien)
- a numeral and its unit in measurements, time or date (eg 33 mL, 3 pm, 55 BCE)
- two SI units used in combination (eg 3 N m (Newton metres), 11 m s (metres per second))
- one, two or three digits attached to a word or abbreviation (eg Henry VIII, £3 million)
- one, two or three characters that form part of a reference (eg Fig. 12, Ex. A, MS Harley 4866)
- p, pp, fo./fol. or similar and the page/folio number(s) (eg p 7, fols 3^v–4^r)
- an abbreviation and any characters to which it is attached (eg Dr No, & Co.)
- copyright symbol and copyright owner (eg © Jane Smith).

On a PC or Mac keyboard, Ctrl + Shift + Spacebar produces a standard non-breaking space in MS Word.

Spacing around punctuation

The commonest punctuation marks are typically closed up to the preceding character and followed by a single space. The main exceptions to these two conventions are the apostrophe, dashes and the enclosure marks: parentheses, brackets, curly braces and quotation marks.

> Villon is remembered for *les neiges d'antan* ('the snows of yester-year' in Rossetti's translation).

Stops (if used) in abbreviations are usually closed up on both sides (e.g., a.m.), and personal initials can be closed up, depending on style.

Final stops are closed up to the preceding character and followed by a single space. Whereas a double space between sentences improved the readability of documents produced on typewriters with a fixed (non-proportional) font such as Courier, with proportional fonts double spaces are a distraction and waste space, so this practice is now actively discouraged. Indeed, in April 2020, MS Word began flagging a double space after a full stop as an error.

Quotation marks are closed up to the quoted matter, but this was not always so. In British publishing, especially fiction, quotes (also semicolons and colons) were spaced until the 1950s.

Vertical lists

Vertical lists, such as shopping lists, menus or to-do lists, are punctuated by spacing and layout, and may not need any other punctuation. It is not easy to grasp complex information in a run-on list:

> Maastricht categories are I. Found dead (uncontrolled), either I.A out of hospital or I.B in hospital; II. Witnessed cardiac arrest (uncontrolled), either II.A out of hospital or II.B in hospital; III. Withdrawal of life-sustaining therapy (controlled DCD); IV. Cardiac arrest while brain-dead (uncontrolled or controlled).

A vertical list makes the information much easier to take in, almost at a glance:

> Maastricht categories are
>
> I. Found dead (uncontrolled)
>   I.A out of hospital
>   I.B in hospital
> II. Witnessed cardiac arrest (uncontrolled)
>   II.A out of hospital
>   II.B in hospital
> III. Withdrawal of life-sustaining therapy (controlled DCD)
> IV. Cardiac arrest while brain-dead (uncontrolled or controlled).

Where the run-on list was punctuated by commas and semicolons, and further articulated by 'either ... or', the vertical list is punctuated by a new line for each item.

Some styles would add a colon after the introduction ('Maastricht categories are'); some styles would omit both that colon and the final stop. Because each element of a vertical list starts on a new line, this usually results in more white space before the line end, which makes the list easier to read. Turnover lines can be further indented on the left, helping to clarify where a new item begins.

Vertical lists can eliminate ambiguity in complex lists, especially those containing sublists.

> The minister proposed a new scheme to build capacity, particularly in less developed regions, to promote gender equality; improve existing support, identifying opportunities for synergy with local NGOs; and devise multi-agency strategies; and make better use of existing capacity.

A sentence like this forces us to re-read and even then leaves us unsure what it is trying to say. Is the scheme going to promote and devise? Or will it only build capacity? A vertical list is not only much clearer but also quicker to review in case of doubt.

> The minister proposed a new scheme to
>
> - build capacity, particularly in less developed regions, to:
>   » promote gender equality
>   » improve existing support, identifying opportunities for synergy with local NGOs
>   » devise multi-agency strategies
> - make better use of existing capacity.

For punctuation, vertical lists are often indented from the left and typically use bullets, with hollow bullets or arrows for sublists, which are further indented at each level of sublist. Where a list shows order of importance or a sequence that must be followed, or where other text refers to items in the list, it should use numbers (arabic, with roman for sublists) or letters (which can be upper case, with lower case for sublists). A vertical list is also spaced above and below by leading.

If all information of the same kind is presented in vertical lists, it may be a good idea to follow this style even for lists that have only two items. However, a vertical list with one item would be decidedly odd.

Bibliographies and reference lists are a special kind of vertical list. They use abbreviations and omit stops and spaces to compress a lot of information into a small space, so each entry needs space around it in the form of leading and/or a hanging indent. A list (or table) of contents follows a similar pattern.

Indexes are also a special type of vertical list, in which the headings each start on a new line, with subheads either run on (after a colon, with further subheads separated by semicolons) or set out (each indented, on a new line with a hanging indent, with each level of subhead further indented). If there are two or more levels of subhead, the index is best set out. Spacing is important in indexes, and the hanging indent for a turnover line must be clearly distinguished from the indent for a lower level of subhead (or for a cross-reference where this is given a separate line). The indexer should be asked to check the proofs.

Another obscure fact

In some typefaces, italic and roman spaces are visibly different in width. Try it for yourself, using various fonts in Word. Proofreaders need to be able to spot such discrepancies.

9 | Where now?

Expensive punctuation

Legal documents are very lightly punctuated, and poor punctuation can have serious consequences in a court of law. There have been many cases where missing or misinterpreted commas have cost companies millions.[2] In the 2017 case of *O'Connor v. Oakhurst Dairy*, the dairy in Maine – relying on an ambiguously punctuated statute – ended up having to pay $5 million to its lorry drivers, who had not been paid overtime. A comma in the wrong place in the 1872 US Tariff Act lost the government $2 million in tax, and another cost Lockheed Martin Aerospace $70 million in underpriced aircraft.

Writers and editors who work on books that include legal precedents need to be very cautious about changes to punctuation. If the text includes a draft clause or sample contract that lawyers can use as an example to follow, it is important not to change it at all, even to add commas that seem obviously needed.

It is not just money that can be lost through questions of punctuation. Evidence in the investigation of the murder of Stephen Lawrence was disregarded because the punctuation was mistranscribed, and although it is not true that Sir Roger Casement was hanged by a comma, his lawyer did attempt to defend him on the basis of a comma in the 1351 Treason Act.

Changing practice

In the first proofreading manual (Leipzig, 1608), Jerome Hornschuch wrote (in Latin, of course):

---

[2] listverse.com/2015/09/12/10-simple-typos-with-surprisingly-huge-costs.

> Correct punctuation produces great elegance and leads more than anything else to a clear understanding of the subject-matter.
>
> Jerome Hornschuch, *Orthotypographia*, trans. P Gaskell and P Bradford

What is 'correct' will vary with the content and the context, from person to person and place to place, from time to time and age to age. That is because punctuation is a language, so it has to make sense to the reader. That is why this guide is relentlessly reasonable, with guidance based on reasons that I hope make sense, and not on rules.

Punctuation has evolved to give a high degree of clarity, subtlety and flexibility, but everyone has their own taste and practice. To one person, hyphens clarify; to another, hyphens look fussy. No commas at all may please lawyers but baffle lay readers; too many commas will slow down every reader. In a minimalist age, commas and hyphens may be eliminated as too fussy. That may please the writer and editor, but they already know what the text means. The readers don't. Even if a text can ultimately be read only one way despite a lack of punctuation, readers may not get it right first time or may not find it easy. We have no right to waste people's time by forcing them to go back and re-read.

> Rules only take us so far.
>
> Kurt Vonnegut, *A Man without a Country* (quoted by David Crystal in *Making a Point*)

What most people write (or see written) will tend to become the norm. In that sense there are no rules; instead, we all contribute to an understanding of what means what in vocabulary, grammar and punctuation. Well-judged editing helps that understanding because if most text that most people see has been well edited, then edited text exemplifies and normalises good punctuation, which is punctuation that reflects the grammar and clarifies the sense.

10 | Resources

This guide sets out as much guidance on British punctuation as most editors and proofreaders will normally need, but *Making a Point* and *New Hart's Rules* between them give the most comprehensive and authoritative advice. Seely's handy A–Z layout covers the basics, with all examples based on updated corpora.

Guides
Essential guides
Judith Butcher, Caroline Drake and Maureen Leach (2014). 6.12 Punctuation. In *Butcher's Copy-Editing*. 4th edn. CUP.

Jeremy Butterfield, ed. (2015). *Fowler's Dictionary of Modern English Usage*. 4th edn. OUP.

John Seely (2020). *Oxford A–Z of Grammar and Punctuation*. 3rd edn. OUP.

Anne Waddingham, ed. (2014). *New Hart's Rules*. 2nd edn. OUP.

Punctuation guides and sources
Vivian Cook. Frequencies for English punctuation marks. **viviancook.uk/Punctuation/PunctFigs.htm**.

David Crystal (2015). *Making a Point: The pernickety story of English punctuation*. Profile Books.

Louise Harnby. Punctuation resources for crime, mystery and thriller writers and fiction editors. **louiseharnbyproofreader.com/punctuation.html**.

Older guides with useful insights
Bas Aarts (2011). *Oxford Modern English Grammar*. OUP.

Gordon V Carey (1976). *Mind the Stop: A brief guide to punctuation*. Rev. edn. Penguin.

Ernest Gowers (2014). *Plain Words: A guide to the use of English*. Rev. edn. Particular Books.

Eric Partridge (1999). *You Have a Point There: A guide to punctuation and its allies.* Routledge.

Larry Trask (1997). *Penguin Guide to Punctuation.* Penguin. Also available online at **sussex.ac.uk/informatics/punctuation.**

Training courses
Proofreading

Punctuation is a major element in proofreading courses, which CIEP offers at three levels:

Proofreading 1: Introduction

Proofreading 2: Headway

Proofreading 3: Progress

ciep.uk/training/choose-a-course/proofreading-suite-courses

We also recommend the Publishing Training Centre (PTC) course Essential Proofreading.

publishingtrainingcentre.co.uk/courses/self-study/tutor-guided-courses/essential-proofreading-editorial-skills-one

Grammar and punctuation

This CIEP course alternates units on grammar and punctuation, based on practice among users of British English but also highlighting some differences in American English.

ciep.uk/training/choose-a-course/getting-to-grips-grammar-punctuation

11 | Glossary

adjectival phrase: a phrase headed by an adjective.

adverbial [noun]: an optional phrase or clause that extends the meaning of the verb, eg *as soon as I arrived*, he began complaining.

apposition: of two noun phrases referring to the same person or thing in different terms, eg *Norma Whitcombe, the progenitor of the SfEP*.

attributive: of an adjectival phrase preceding a noun (or noun phrase).

clause: a phrase that contains a subject and a verb.

complement: a phrase or clause that is needed to complete the meaning (usually of a verb), eg It sounds *a little odd*.

coordinating conjunctions: *and*, *but* and *or* join similar elements in a sentence.

defining (restrictive) relative clause: a clause that defines what (or whom) we are referring to, eg the man *that I love*.

dependent clause: see **subordinate clause**, eg *that I love*.

direct object: the thing or person targeted by the verb, eg I baked *a cake* (where *a cake* was the thing baked; we can sometimes add an indirect object, eg I baked *her* a cake).

gerund: the *-ing* form of a verb used as a noun (though it is not always analysed like that), eg my hobbies are *reading* and *thinking*.

gloss: a definition, clarification and/or explanation.

indentation: a fixed space between the margin and the text.

independent clause: a clause that can stand alone, eg *they didn't believe me*.

leading: (said 'ledding') interline spacing, originally strips of lead used to put space between lines of type.

minimal capitals: (usually *min. caps*) using upper case only for the first word (in a title or sentence) and for names.

non-breaking space: a space on screen that cannot be broken by a line end, eg between number and unit in *33 mg*.

noun phrase: two or more words that together function as a noun, eg *don't knows*.

object: see **direct object**.

phrase: two or more words that are seen as a unit.

predicate: a verb and those parts of the sentence that go with the verb.

rhetoric: the art of persuasion.

roman: normal (upright) type, as opposed to *italic*.

sentence: a clause (along with other clauses or phrases) that makes complete sense by itself.

serial comma (Oxford comma): a comma always placed before *and* or *or* at the end of a list, regardless of sense.

subject: the subject of a verb is the actor or protagonist, eg *birds* fly over the rainbow – though sometimes only notionally, eg *it* is raining.

subordinate clause: a clause that cannot stand alone, eg *that I love*.

subordinating conjunctions: *because, when, if only* and several more such conjunctions introduce a subordinate clause.

syntactic bond: a link between two words that cannot be separated because they combine to give the meaning.

syntax: the conventions that govern the arrangement of words into sentences.

terms of art: words and phrases that have a narrow or specific meaning to a specialist (in any 'art'), eg *morbidity rates* measure the extent of disease, not how gloomy the patients are.

About the author

After some years teaching and many more driving heavy lorries, **Gerard M-F Hill** retrained to work with words. Since 1990 he has worked on over 500 books as copyeditor, indexer, proofreader or writer. As a director of SfEP (2007–16) he devised the basic editorial test used by the CIEP, and as chartership adviser (2016–20) he worked with the then chair, Sabine Citron, to obtain the Institute's Royal Charter. He has mentored 120 proofreaders and devised online courses, including The Art of Querying (CIEP 2021). He lives and works in an old chapel on a hillside in breezy Cumberland, but then someone has to.

much-better-text.com

Acknowledgements

Even if they never really believe it, every author needs an editor. So I am very grateful to **Margaret Hunter**, the information director who commissioned this guide and got more than she bargained for. She gave me the chance to think further about punctuation, she kept faith with this guide even after discovering that it was twice the length she had expected. She and information editor **Cathy Tingle** gave it added value even when they kept suggesting cuts. Without their help it would have been finished in half the time – and been full of faults. My warm thanks go to them and the rest of the editorial team, who worked assiduously to suggest improvements and find the typos, gaps and errors that I unaccountably missed. I also wish to thank the beta readers, namely

Emily Haag, Entry-Level Member of the CIEP
polishedpeneditorial.co.uk

Jane Hammett, Advanced Professional Member of the CIEP
jane-hammett.co.uk

who both gave positive feedback while gently pointing out infelicities. No prizes are offered for spotting any that remain, but readers may be sure they are all the fault of the author.

www.ingramcontent.com/pod-product-compliance
Lightning Source LLC
Chambersburg PA
CBHW040419100526
44588CB00022B/2876